SPACE SONGS

Myra Cohn Livingston, Poet

Leonard Everett Fisher, Painter

SCHOLASTIC INC.
New York   Toronto   London   Auckland   Sydney

For Nicolas Alan Brugge

Myra Cohn Livingston would like to thank retired professor Lloyd Motz, Department of Astronomy, Columbia University, for evaluating the text.

CONTENTS

OTHERWHERE

Space is an other world,

an otherwhere.

Night-watchman moon guards darkness.

One by one,

lanterns blink on.

Stars pinwheel the Milky Way.

Planets spin and journey.

Comets tumble there.

Asteroids hide in ice-clouds.

Sizzling sun,

festooned in loops of fire,

brings back day.

MESSAGES

Space sends messages,
    mysterious sounds:

        Pulsing beats
        from distant
        neutron stars;

Radio blackouts from a solar flare;

    Hissing meteorites
        thundering
          the
            ground;

Signals from puzzling quasars;

        Small,
        strange
        whistlers
        from
        Jupiter.

MILKY WAY

Here, where old halo stars and sun were birthed,

Here, where stars huddle together in interstellar clouds,

Here, where hot new stars are born and supernovae die;

Nourished on dust and gas, shining on earth,

Two hundred billion stars move here in teeming crowds.

Here is the Milky Way, our galaxy, our dusky road in sky.

Moon remembers.

Marooned in shadowed night,

white powder plastered
on her pockmarked face,
scarred with craters,
filled with waterless seas,

she thinks back
to the Eagle,
to the flight
of men from Earth,
of rocks sent back in space,
and one
faint
footprint
in the Sea of Tranquility.

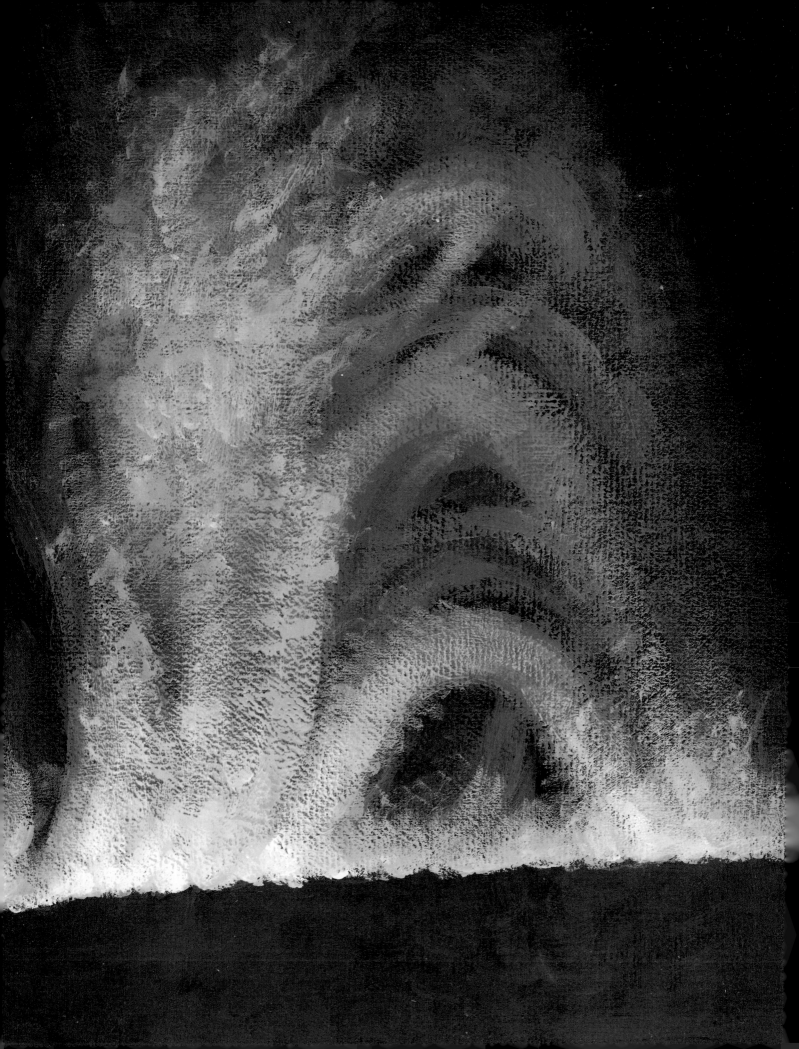

Space
is afire
with bursts of bubbling gas,

colliding atoms,
boiling wells
and solar flares

spewing

from a burning star, the sun.

Ninety-three million miles away

this mass,
quaking inferno,
pluming arcs and bridges

roars;

a giant bomb
exploding
hydrogen.

JEWELS

Space blazes with jewels,
    a shimmering ice
    of billions of diamonds
  dazzle
    the Milky Way:

      Jupiter, a giant agate,

    Uranus, a ball of jade,

      Pluto, a luminescent pearl,

Saturn, a halo of rings.

      A slice
    of moon, a crescent brooch.

  Bright rubies splay
  Antares

    in this
      midnight
     masquerade.

METEORITES

Tales that they tell are true
of falling stars from otherwhere;
of fireballs, of meteorites,
of lumps of rock and metal crashing down;
of stones and stony-irons from afar.
Earthlings may watch a meteor's blazing trail of light.

Earthlings may find its fragments on the ground.

Long distance travelers
from the cold
of space,
ice-clad,
dirty,
tugged by a passing star,

journey to see the sun
whose searing burn
swells them with gas
as on they race

streaming their blowing, sunlit hair.

These are comets.
They come.
They go.

They will return.

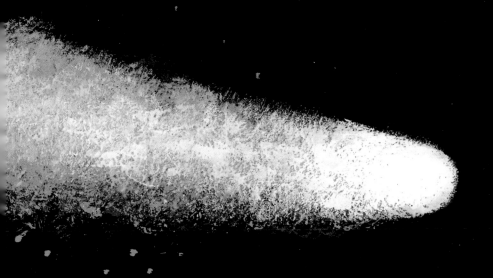

Space is a

playing field for asteroids.

Dusty and sun-scorched,
orbiting
about the sun,
each has a name:
      Eros,
      Icarus,
      Vesta,
      Flora . . .
Through a great void
these chunks
of rock
and metal
run,
    hurtling,
        colliding

in their endless game.

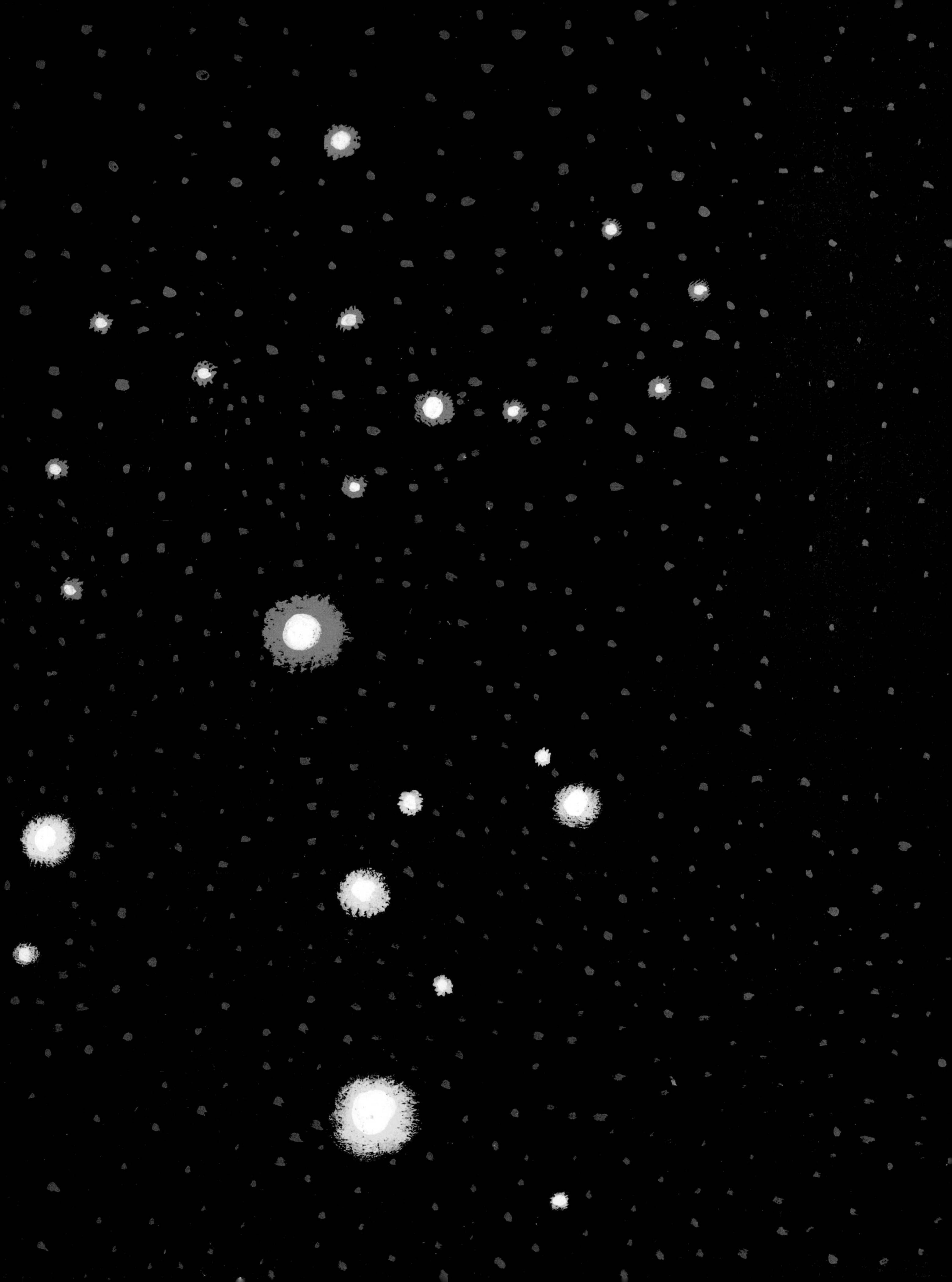

STARS AND CONSTELLATIONS

The Seven Sisters
sail up in the sky.

Virgo,
Pisces,
Leo
cluster there.

White,
yellow,
red,
blue,

these luminous spheres
glow gases,

crowd
in fuzzy nebulae,

cold clouds
and constellations.

Dwarfs,
giants,
supernovae

glare   from space.

All these we call our stars.

SATELLITES

Monitors of steel,
these space detectives seek
clues to the beginning of our galaxy.
Informers of the energy of stars, of gamma rays;
weighted with sensors,
They listen, watch, and speak
of radiation, solar flares,
atmospheric density.

Stalking magnetic fields,

they serve out their days.

Space keeps its secrets
hidden.

It does not tell.

Are black holes time machines?
Where do lost comets go?

Is Pluto moon or planet?

How many, how vast
unknown galaxies beyond us?

Do other creatures
dwell   on distant spheres?

Will we ever know?

Space is silent.

It seldom answers.

But we ask.

Space is a kaleidoscope,
a shifting dream
of sphere and shape;

Each realm, each body
named
on Earth,
transfigured in the sky.

Dazzled by light,
by a resplendent beam,

some soar skyward,
some go up in flame,

like stars and starstuff,
born to live,
to blaze,
and die.

ISBN 0-590-44489-1

Copyright © 1988 by Myra Cohn Livingston.
Illustrations copyright © 1988 by Leonard Everett Fisher.
All rights reserved. Published by Scholastic Inc.,
730 Broadway, New York, NY 10003, by arrangement with
Holiday House.

12 11 10 9 8 7 6   9/9 0 1 2/0

Printed in the U.S.A.   08

First Scholastic printing, March 1991